WHEN A WOMAN'S BROKEN

LASHEA HETHERINGTON

Copyright © 2026 Lashea Hetherington

Published by CaryPress International Books
www.carypress.com

All rights reserved. No part of this publication may be reproduced, distributed, or transmitted in any form or by any means, including photocopying, recording, or other electronic or mechanical methods, without the prior written permission of the publisher, except in the case of brief quotations embodied in critical reviews and certain other non-commercial uses permitted by copyright law.

TABLE OF CONTENTS

Main Characters 1

Preface 3

The Cycle of Dysfunction 9

Distress 11

My Escape 17

Summer, 2016 21

The Next 27

My dream 29

Where is God 33

Bomb Dropped 35

My daughters 37

How do you regroup 39

Just imagine 41

My mother 43

Through it all 45

The Pain 47

Faith	49
Therapy	51
Disposable	53
Strength	55
War of Love	57
Got my Mojo Back	59
Meeting The Love of My Life	61
Affliction!	65
Thinking	69
I refuse to be broken	71
Guess who's back?	73
I'm glad I'm still standing	75

MAIN CHARACTERS

Marjorie (Mom) – She is a tall, beautiful woman with olive skin and brown eyes. She is in her early sixties with a ton of experience about motherhood and love. She played a major role in my life as a young woman. She was close enough to show me the ropes of life, knotty ropes though. She showed me how to take care of my family, with love, loyalty, and support, and also how to be a loving wife. A reality I embraced and lived but never experienced.

Simon (Dad) - People say I get my face from my dad. I wouldn't disagree. His round face, tight jawline, and straight nose never really gave away his exact age, impressive for a man in his late sixties. Throughout my journey, I saw different sides of my dad, something you'll get to see as well. He stands out as a provider, a disciplined man, and a great-grandfather to my children.

Joseph (Daughters' Dad)- The saying *"you fall in love with someone like your father"* is supposed to be a myth. I wished it were just that, a myth. The young man I fell in love with turned out to be the younger version of my dad, a Wreck-It-Ralph kind of character. Now, I remember him as a father to my two beautiful daughters, a hustler, and a memory.

Randall (Ex-fiancé)- When love comes knocking in the form of a 34-year-old young man with a handsome face and charming personality, the door swings open to embrace it. Yeah, don't do that. Even the devil wears beautiful robes with a pretty face.

Jason (The love of my life)- I chose differently. Rather than a man with a tall build and a chiseled face, I chose a friendly and cute face. He was a good friend, a kind soul, and an excellent conversationalist. I found love in an unlikely place, and it blossomed into something sweet and passionate. Did it last though?

PREFACE

1 Corinthians 13: 4-5 Love endures with patience and serenity, love is kind and thoughtful, and is not jealous or envious; love does not brag and is not proud or arrogant. Love is not rude or self-seeking, it is not easily angered, nor takes into account wrong endured.

This is the love I read of. The love I yearned for.

Growing up in a two-parent household presented me with my first experience of what love looks like. Based on the length of my parents' marriage, I assumed along the way that they were doing something right. The part they played in their lives was clearly defined: Dad paid the bills and took care of us financially, while Mom made the home. To me, this was what love was supposed to look like, feel like.

My father was a great father, a provider. As I got older, I would ask him questions about guys, how they think, operate, and why men just do certain things, because I wanted to see if I was the problem. How can I conform to being loved? My dad didn't have much to say because, guess what, he was looking at himself in the mirror because of the dialogue we would have. He was stuck; he could only answer to the level he was delivered from. I love and respect my dad because that is who God chose, but I didn't respect how he treated my mother. She deserved better, while my dad and I have a great relationship. My prayer is that he gives my mother the love that she deserves before she leaves this earth.

I saw my mom being rejected time after time by her husband, as she continued to fight for love. She stayed in a 38-year-old marriage without experiencing passionate love, was never held right or appreciated for her labors. She slowly became the 'angry black woman' without realizing it. I never really understood her till I got into my first relationship at 19. Neither the love I grew up with nor experienced reflected the definition of love in 1 Corinthian 13: 4-5.

I believe I am not the only woman with this experience.

This is why I am sharing my story with you. Healing can be found for everyone who has experienced heartbreak in a toxic relationship. I had questions all through the healing process, some of which you might have. Rejection, after rejection, what do you do with yourself? How do you pick yourself back up? How do you recover from so many rejections? Why endure so much pain in the name of love, even when you are shattered like a million pieces of glass lying on the floor and not sure which way to go? Why can't I be valued in the name of love? Why do I always get tossed to the side? Why do I get tossed like I'm disposable?

Talking to friends and family about romantic relationships becomes exhausting because it feels embarrassing and overwhelmingly painful. They say, 'stop picking, stop going there, get you somebody different.' It looks as though you are desperate to have a man and will do anything just to be loved and accepted, even if it's the wrong love. What do you do when you have a hole in your soul? What do you do when you have been constantly rejected by someone you loved wholly?

If you have these kinds of questions, this book is for you. This book is for the woman who has been broken after a relationship that was supposed to last or change for the better. By faith in Christ Jesus, let's experience healing and wholeness as God's children.

What do you do when your first relationship at the age of 19 was for 11 years of turmoil and toxic love, then get back in another relationship for 5 years and experience the same? Also, when Mom showed you to stay in a marriage/relationship through thick and thin. But it still is dysfunctional, and she stays there in the name of love, loyalty, but what do you do when you have dysfunctional loyalty because you have hope, you made a vow to God and your husband, but your needs of being loved properly and healthily are not going in the right direction?

As a 38-year-old woman, I have been broken so many times by this thing called "love". It has broken me to the point of shattering my heart into a million pieces. Why do I feel I'm the only woman in the world who has endured so many rejections from men that I had an interest in or loved? How can you regroup from so many broken pieces of your heart that have been shattered when people look at you and say, 'Why is she not married yet? Why can't she keep a man? What is wrong with her?'

Then how can you manage not to become bitter, miserable, angry, and not trusting? How do you protect your soul and spirit on top of wanting to still be loved correctly and have a healthy marriage? When all you have experienced in the name of love, rejection, and brokenness is all you can identify with. How can you trust the name of love in people? Can you see a clear vision of real love when all you know, see, and experience is rejection? You continue to fight for the true meaning of love and pure love, not tainted, dysfunctional love.

The level of pain, rejection, and abuse within a short period of time, so that's 18 years of three relationships before the age of 40 rejection, rejection, rejection. Once again, how do you still have faith in love and God? How do you not give up or throw in the towel? How do you keep yourself from jumping off a bridge or a cliff?

Time after time, in between the 18 years of broken love, where can you find healing? Do you think that accepting the behavior of dysfunctional love makes you weak? Do you think that a person will change over time, so you decide to stay around? How much more can a woman endure in the name of love, but also tainted love?

There is purpose and healing in the hurt that has been inflicted upon you. You could have been molested, not getting treated the right way, by a mother or father. I just have one question: do you want to be healed, delivered, and set free, or do you want to be stuck in the pain of someone else not loving you properly?

When growing up as a little girl, you have fairytales or visions of your life, how it's going to go. One thing I learned through therapy is that we can't go through life without any hardships or trials and tribulations. It's inevitable, when hardship comes, it births character and patience, and also changes your lens on life.

THE CYCLE OF DYSFUNCTION

From the moment I clocked 18, I started fantasizing about marriage. I grew up in a family of five; there's my dad, my mom, my sister, my brother, and I. As the first daughter, I was groomed to be an excellent wife and mother for my future children and husband. Sitting with my mom on random evenings gave me a chance to listen to her own story about what marriage felt like. It didn't strike me as the best out there, but I thought it lasted this long, right?

My mom shared stories that never felt right. My dad always maintained a stoic personality throughout my childhood, but showed my mom his emotional side negatively. She endured emotional and verbal abuse in the 38-year-long marriage. It came as insults, sharp, unwarranted remarks about her appearance, and many things I never picked up on as a young child. A cycle of dysfunction was created in my little family, a loop I got caught in.

I developed an interest in reading fictional romance stories, which filled my head with different ideas of what love looked like. A sweet kind with a happy ending and a thriving family. When I thought of marriage as an 18-year-old, I dreamt of a love that melts me into a puddle of beautiful emotions. As I get older and experience life, my perspective has changed. My only prayer for marriage was that my love story would be wholesome and totally different from what my mom experienced.

DISTRESS

August 12, 2002

On this very day, I met Joseph at the grocery store while I was trying to buy ice cream. I remember craving it so badly that I left the house to get it at 9 p.m, something my 19-year-old self wouldn't do ordinarily. The blue shirt he had on made his face look friendly and kind. His first words to me were, "Do you stare at guys a lot?" I caught myself stealing glances at him from the frozen foods section. It was a simple way of signaling *"hey, I like what I see"*. Looking back, it was naïve of me, but it got the job done because two days later, we went on our first date.

A few years down the line, I fell deeply in love with the man I had briefly gotten acquainted with. The cycle of dysfunction began to unload when I found out about the kind of job he did. He was a drug dealer in the neighborhood. It brought in cash for our daily expenses and a little more, but I started getting nervous. That lifestyle was unknown to me because I didn't grow up that way. The rough side of Joseph crept out slowly, and I, unfortunately, was on the receiving end. He became verbally and physically violent with me for trivial reasons, and at times there was no reason at all.

It became more frequent after the birth of my first daughter. During postpartum, my mom discovered the situation I was going through. I was never comfortable with the constant abuse, but I was so deeply embarrassed by the situation that I never shared it with anyone. My mom went off on him, protected me, and consoled me, but I wanted to stay with him.

Being raised in a black community presents you with different experiences, but one thing we are made to understand is loyalty. I do not intend to generalize, but from observation, we are not really taught how to have healthy boundaries in a romantic relationship. Healthy and nurturing love takes time and effort because it doesn't come naturally; it is usually an experience many people in the community miss out on. I did, and so did my parents. As time goes by, we unintentionally continue the cycle of dysfunction and raise children who are unaware of what healthy relationships are supposed to look like.

After our little talk that day, I realized that I had to work towards having a better relationship for myself. At least, I could try everything my mom suggested. You'd think that is the proper way of showing love, but it only kept me at the mercy of Joseph, experiencing mental abuse, verbal abuse, and physical abuse. This is not love, but because it was all I had ever known for so many years, there was nothing else I could do.

I looked at my life at a standstill at the age of 25 and asked, *What is next?*

I fell pregnant with my second child while in a toxic relationship, so I kept her. It hadn't gotten to the hilt for me, so I gave a little more love to my family, to Joseph. I knew I wanted a different and healthy relationship, but I decided to stay with my children's father for another 5 years. Well, that was tormenting because the whole 5 years were another vicious cycle of hurt and pain, verbal and mental abuse, and more physical abuse.

Experiencing Joseph (both of my daughters' father) made me realize that I endured the same kind of mental and verbal abuse as my mother endured from my father. The cycle of dysfunction that had already begun kept me from experiencing something different and new. I ended up having 2 children in the 11-year relationship I shared with Joseph.

By 25, I didn't want to keep this vicious cycle of dysfunctional love because I was showing my daughters how to make the same mistakes without showing them something better to hope for. I just didn't know how to go about leaving this man that I loved to the depths of my heart.

By the time I was 30 years old, I ended up getting pregnant the third time while I stayed with Joseph. I began to ask necessary questions like, do I really want to have a third child with this guy? Do I want to continue this relationship? Do I want to repeat the same troubles I saw my mom endure while I was a little girl? I thought about the impact it would have on my daughters and the one currently on the way.

I was practically a single mother while I had Joseph with me because I was not helped with raising my children. During this period, I was so consumed with my responsibilities at home that I de-prioritized my relationship with God. So, my relationship with God did not flourish. I had no time to do any praying or study of the Word. I just looked at my life and my daughter's life. I don't want to do this again, a third time, then I made the decision to abort the baby. I was 2 months pregnant, and I honestly felt it was a relief. I was hurt that I aborted my baby, but I didn't want to bring another child into this world to suffer or even experience the torment of their parents. I took a stand and fought for my peace and my dignity. Before I reached the age of 31, the relationship with Joseph was over.

MY ESCAPE

February 15, 2013

I had the abortion scheduled the moment I found out I was pregnant, without letting Joseph know. I didn't tell my parents or my siblings because they would have advised against it. Truthfully, they could have supported my decision but I didn't want to give anybody a chance to change my mind. I had suffered enough; I didn't want to lead that life with Joseph anymore because I began to believe that I could get someone better. I just had to close one door for another to open.

I got a handful of jobs in home care to save up a cushion fund for my daughters and I. I needed my own money, without him knowing. The shift was tough because I needed to take my daughters out of that community entirely and set them up in a new school, a new house, and a new neighborhood. This was my chance to start a new life, away from all I have ever known.

I scraped by and took extra shifts so I could meet my goals before the end of 2013. My daughters had to stay with my parents while I worked because I could never leave them alone with Joseph. Not because he was violent or inappropriate toward them, but because he sold drugs. I don't ever want them to use the substance or get hooked. I had enough problems, so I never went into the rabbit hole of addiction. I don't want my daughters to experience a fresh set of problems because of my mistakes. So, the choice was personal and meant to protect them.

During this period, my dad got closer with my daughters. He was gentle and attentive towards them. My daughters would tell me many things they did with their grandfather while I was away at work. It sparked a bit of hope for my strained relationship with my dad. Still, I couldn't tell anyone my plans. I gathered my earnings after working for 6 months and left the community while Joseph was away on business. I left in the middle of the night when no one could stop me. I had my things packed up and got a friend to drive me out to my new beginning. I knew it was going to be hard for my daughters and I, but I was willing to give us a fighting chance.

Three months after my 11-year relationship ended, I felt as though I was set free. The crippling anxiety that always accompanied me while I was with Joseph slowly crept away. I didn't expect it, but I saw my daughters smile more freely and happily. Nothing could have prepared me for this realization; I unconsciously kept my daughters locked up with me in a cycle of abuse and dysfunctionality. Abuse never affects only the targeted victim; it spreads towards everything and everyone in that vicinity, just like it did when I was with my parents.

Slowly, my life was constantly filled with color and happiness.

Three years after my escape, I felt like I was ready for something new. After all, I left the old to experience newness and then I met Randall.

SUMMER, 2016

July, 2016

I started easing into my new life with my daughters as things slowly fell into place. I experienced casual flirting with some, but being a single mother threw them off. Regardless, I invested in my appearance and joined a gym. I had to keep my mind sharp and body active while I worked to make sure my daughters had the best. I made friends with some ladies at the gym, and they slowly became my own community (my girls). It became easier to share my troubles and little hiccups because they gave me support without heavy judgment.

September, 2016

I was at the bar with some of my girls late in the evening when I felt a gentle tap on my shoulder. Sweat trickled down the deep neckline of my pink floral top. I had a number of *what-ifs* rolling in my head. What if Joseph found me and wanted his daughters back? What if he made a scene?

I slowly turned around in that minute, and I was met with the most beautiful smile I had ever seen. It was a bit flirty too, but who cares? The loud music at the bar made me keep a close contact with this handsome guy. We had to speak into each other's ears to maintain the small, flirty conversation we had going on. Randall nudged me to dance with him, and I obliged. A few nights passed, and I was intrigued by this charming man who I spoke to every night after I tucked my daughters in.

It turned out that one of the ladies brought Randall to meet me in hopes that we would hit it off. He had all the simple qualities I desired in a man. He worked, paid his bills, had his own place, and had a charming personality. During one of our late-night talks, he told me he had a son that he was taking care of. It was then that I summoned up the courage to tell him about my daughters. He told me he had no issues with it and was interested in me. We took our friendship to the next level and started a committed relationship a few weeks after the prior conversation. We would do family dinners, trips, and go out with other couples, just as I always wanted.

I had the best period with Randall because he made me feel seen and loved in ways I had never experienced before. Cumulatively, our relationship lasted for five years, and it had its own share of troubles, some of which I never anticipated. It wasn't a straight five years; we broke up and got back together in between the five years.

We would stop talking to each other because of disagreements, the disagreements would be mainly because he didn't understand me, he was controlling, and wanted the relationship to go his way. But because I have been through so much turmoil with my daughter's dad, I didn't put up with his behavior. He would get mad and say that I don't fight for us. I argued that I do, but I'm not lowering my standards or my worth because he wants everything to go his way.

He did have the potential of being a great man and husband. Fast forward to 2018. He decided to propose to me via text. I waited a couple of days to respond, and then I gave him a yes. He was so excited, and in the midst of that, I was in the process of buying my first home. This year is the time when we broke up for a 6-month hiatus, so we got back together.

I remember I was in the car, on the phone with him. His energy was off, and I felt different, so I knew something was wrong. I said Are you ok? He was very quiet. I said What is wrong? What, you don't want to be with me anymore?

He said I love you, I would never say that. I said, What is wrong? Immediately, I felt like God dropped it in my spirit so loud and clear. So, I said, Who did you get pregnant? It turned out that he had a thing with another woman during our split, and it resulted in a break-up baby. I told him I said you are pursuing two different women, and you don't know who to choose. The phone was so quiet for a few minutes, and I was so sick to my stomach. That is part of the reason why he proposed to me, I guess.

Randall apologised profusely. He said, Can we work this out? I don't want to lose you. I was torn by the recent developments. Needless to say, I proceeded with the engagement. About 3 months later, he called the engagement off because we were not seeing eye to eye about me buying my house. He wanted me to give up my home to move in with him. I promise God didn't allow that, but I gave him certain solutions for us to continue our engagement. He turned them down because he wanted things to go his way.

During that downtime after he called off the engagement, I heard whispers from God about being Mrs. J (Randall's last name) and another dream about Randall proposing to me. These combined influenced me to stay a little longer. Honestly, he was different from what I had just come from. I liked him a lot, for one. He respected and took care of his mother and worked, so that was a plus. But it wasn't built to last because I was rejected, and another was preferred.

After that, once again I was left feeling unworthy. Did I do something wrong? What else could I have done to make it work? I grieved that relationship for six months, just asking why can't I get the love I deserve and need. Fast forward, and he comes back in 2019, tries again, and it still doesn't work out. We started to argue too much. In the midst of our breakup, he ended up being with another female, so I was basically the side chick for a little while.

I was trying to get my spot back! How can you choose someone else after wanting to marry me multiple times? Why would you give her the benefit of the doubt instead of giving us another chance at marriage? Why would you give her more value after all that we had been through together? I could not wrap my head around it, so I stuck around.

Well, he chose her. Once again, I'm back in the hole because I'm over here single and he's in a relationship. I felt as though I would never be loved, that I would never get what I deserve and desire. I felt I had a curse on my love life. Why do I end up with the back end of the stick of love? Why can't I win? Everyone that I know is married, having children, and I'm over here broken, depressed, not knowing my worth anymore. I asked God why, why can't I get what I desire, a relationship, and I'm single. Why did I have to suffer? I know I'm an amazing woman, but I have experienced more losses than wins in the name of love.

Needless to say, I was plain rejected by him. His excuse was that I can't give you the love and attention you deserve because we argue too much. I said whoever you get in a relationship with, you are going to argue and have disagreements. Nothing is going to be perfect. Six months later, I saw him on Facebook with the other woman. That was so devastating to me, I felt like an unworthy woman. I said, "How could he give her a chance and not me?" Why wasn't I worthy enough of his love and attention? After dealing with hurt, rejection, and abuse for 11 years, I went through the same ordeal with Randall. I had no words. I was depressed, I questioned God a lot, asking why I'm not worthy of a healthy and genuine love.

THE NEXT

Six months after he went on with another woman, the relationship he chose ended in some type of domestic, so I heard. After his relationship crashed for the first time, Randall kept on calling me and hoped to rekindle a relationship with me. Of course, he came back, and I tried to be his friend while he grieved the loss of his relationship. This happened in the first week of February because we exchanged Valentine's gifts and all. We ended up back in a relationship, and this time, we took it a step further.

I moved in with him.

MY DREAM

I know God speaks to us in different ways. God speaks to me in my dreams and numbers. This was the reason I stayed and held on to my ex because I thought he was going to be my husband. Most of the time when God gives me a dream, it comes to pass and plays out exactly how I saw it, like a vision. Now, I'm questioning God because that dream where Randall proposed had a different outcome in real life. I thought, God can do anything, and he can change the impossible to the possible. Why then would he give me a dream that fed on my desires?

Subconsciously, what you desire is a dream that God gives as a warning or to let you know what to expect later on. What I'm trying to decipher is that God gives us a promise and he gives us a warning. So why did you change the narrative of my story? I pray that before I finish this book, I will have the answers, but it is confusing to me. God will deliver his promise just the way he gives it to you.

When I moved in with Randall, I thought it would be the change of my prayers, the dream come true in what was given to me. Well, the first thing that happened was he was in the process of buying a home, and in that process of buying his home, he was living with me, and I asked him if this is what you wanted to do? He said yes, I mentioned to him, you know, I want to be married soon, he said ok. The day of him signing on his new house was a turn of events, I was supposed to be on the documents of deed, but because we wasn't married, he couldn't put me on the deed he had to either marry me in a week or so or pay over 3 grand to have me on the documents. I cried because I felt it was another block or hindrance to my dream and what I desire. Within those six months that I stayed there with him, it was hell, I was not comfortable, he thought because I wasn't on the documents that I was trying to sabotage the relationship, but I honestly had peace with it because I said the Father is protecting me from something that I don't see at the moment. Remember, I left the home I bought to move in with him, but the Father's hands were on my life, the whole six months that I was there, I didn't sell my house or rent it out, it was divine protection because when all this was happening, the pandemic of COVID hit, that's what saved my house plus the Father. At the end of March, I moved. I told him I was moving out, he was so nonchalant about it and thought I didn't have the strength to leave him, but I did. It wasn't easy.

He claimed that I was not appreciative of his efforts and complained constantly. Eventually, we broke things off in the following years February after a huge fight regarding a Valentine's gift, and I ended up leaving his house with my daughter's stuff. I just thought that some time apart would be the breakthrough that would finally bring us closer, and we would get married. He will finally recognize my worth. I had a great deal of faith in us, needless to say, that didn't last very long; it crumbled.

I moved out after six months of the relationship. That was the hardest thing I've ever had to do. I reminded myself yet again that I have two beautiful daughters looking at me. I'm saying to myself, How do they view their mother? Let me tell you, I was so broken, torn, and shattered into a million and one pieces. This was 17 years of two broken, toxic relationships. I cried out to God in deep pain. I didn't sign up for all this rejection and brokenness. I thought about committing suicide because the pain was so deep.

WHERE IS GOD

After I moved out from living with Randall, I really questioned God. Side note, I stayed connected to God the whole time in the 18 years of my two relationships, but I grew closer to God before my relationship ended with my daughter's dad. But I thought the closer I grew to God, my hardship would get better, but it seems it heightened even more. I was angry with God. I couldn't reach him; my prayers weren't lining up with what my heart desired. But through it all, I had stayed connected to God, I continued to go to church, I attended women's conferences, and stayed connected to the women God divinely connected in my life. Can I tell you this? God was there in the midst of my brokenness, in my great depression, in my feeling unworthy. God's hand was on my life the whole time I wanted to throw in the towel, but I did feel unloved by God, but in the midst of this, I was understanding his unconditional love even though I didn't feel that way, because in God's word:

Deuteronomy 31:8 The word says will never leave you nor forsake you.

I felt he left me and forsaked his love for me because of everything that I endured in the name of love.

Ok, now it's 5 months since I moved out from Randall, I was grieving, but I was also starting to love myself and feel at peace with my decision. It was in July, when he texted me and said he loves me and wants us to get back together, and was ready. I said ok, if this is what you want, then we have to do counseling and have to be married in the next few months. We did counseling, etc. My mentor would say he was my kryptonite, the same as Superman.

September rolls around, it's his birthday month, he decided he wanted to go to Florida for his birthday, I paid for the trip, and etc. A week before we go on his birthday trip, I had his daughter because he had to work night shift, so I had to go to work the next day, I was calling him and he wasnt answering, so the Holy spirt told me to go to his house, I had his daughter with me so I pull up to the house and long and behold he was in a bed with another woman, my savior... it got violent and crazy. I left. I was so torn and broken I wanted to kill him.

BOMB DROPPED

2022

Wow, I'm not sure what God has in store or how my love life is going to turn out. So as I'm writing this book, I received some news that the ex- Randall that I was with for 5 years has gotten up and gotten married to the girl that he was involved with when he called off the engagement in 2018. Man, I'm not sure how to handle this information. I have so many mixed emotions about this situation. How could you marry her, and as I'm writing the book, our breakup is fresh. We have only been apart for seven months.

What is running through my head is, how could you do this? Why did you find every excuse in the book not to marry me, but you decided to marry her? I ask why I wasn't worthy of that love, the marriage. I wanted to call him and cuss him out, go to his house, and cause a whole scene because it hurts. I just digested this information, but it definitely was a bomb dropped. While I'm sitting here, still grieving the 5-year relationship, still healing from all the pain, you decide to marry that woman. As crazy as it sounds, I still have to trust God in the midst of this atomic bomb that just came to my front door step without me looking for the information. Now you see why I said I didn't want to trust God or anyone else. This is some painful stuff.

Fast forward to June 2023, Randall had a mental breakdown, and his mother called me and said Can you please speak to him? He is riding around with a gun and told his wife, *If I was married to Lashea, these problems wouldn't have happened.* He was admitted to the mental hospital because he suffered a mental breakdown.

After the breakdown, apparently, his then-wife had gone to the police about an argument that they had had. She lied to them about some domestic violence to get her to open the gun safe. As he is a felon, he is not allowed to be around any guns, so during another police call after his trip to the mental hospital, he ended up in jail for around 8 months. After all that, his wife finally left him after destroying his life, and I thought, if Randall led me to a heartbreak for this woman, how could he lead a family with me?

MY DAUGHTERS

In the midst of my brokenness, because I was so depressed, I felt that a black cloud was over my life, and I was losing the battle of love. I didn't know my worth anymore. I was a walking broken human-robot. My routine was to continue to be a mother in the midst of my brokenness and try to be strong for my daughters. To be there for them mentally and physically in the midst of this, I just wanted to get in my bed and lay down and not get up, but God didn't allow that. I'm not sure how I would've made it if I didn't have God on my side and my daughters', even though I felt he had left me to be a single mother. I was persistent in showing my daughters strength and faith in the midst of all the brokenness, and when my heart was shattered like fine china.

I didn't trust God or love anymore because of how love did me. My heart is pure, always has been. I have always felt that when you have a pure heart, we get hurt the most because our motives are pure, and we just want genuine, unconditional love. I wanted to have an icebox around my heart because I didn't think anyone deserved my love, just my daughters, family, and friends.

How Do You Regroup

Now, after all the traumatizing love effects, I was trying to figure out how do I regroup and not stay stuck because of people who didn't want me or just plain rejected me. I stayed connected to God, being consistent with him through all of this. I said there has to be better, God has to have something more for me.

Jeremiah 29:11 says the thoughts I have for you are good, not evil.

At the time, it felt evil because I was still thinking to myself why I was not worthy enough. I wanted and desired something better from the 18 years I had endured. What I saw my mother had endured, at this moment in my life, I had no other reason to trust God because everyone else I trusted with my heart had mishandled it. I continued my regrouping phase by learning myself all over again, knowing what makes me happy, learning to accept genuine unconditional love from God and the people he had in my life. To be honest, I wanted to reject their love because my heart wanted the love from the people I wasn't getting it from. Some people think it's backwards, but it's not, it's actually normal. God had to work on me to learn how to love myself, receiving love from him and the people he had connected to me.

JUST IMAGINE

Just imagine growing up and you've seen dysfunctional love and no growth in your parents' marriage, then your first relationship was the same as what you grew up in. How do you handle that?

I honestly didn't know that I was in the same generational curse. Cycling until I was 25, I started seeing the same behavior in my life. Then you start to question what this is. When I was young, all I knew and witnessed was to stick around and bear the pain, but I knew deep down inside that this wasn't right. I just wanted to stay around because it was my daughter's dad, and I loved him so much, but I was being treated terribly, and I just wanted to be loved.

I wanted him to change, but I didn't know my worth. I thought this was love, and he loved me the best way he knew how. But I knew eventually I had to remove myself, but it was hard, I had to call the cops, and I knew when I went to that extreme, it was over.

MY MOTHER

I often didn't know that I was carrying the weight of my mother's hurt and pain until I experienced it for myself. As God said, 'Daughter, sometimes we have to be the first partakers of our parents' love life just so we can identify and be better." I never viewed my mother as being weak; I just viewed her as: I'm a wife and a mother, so I'm going to fight for my marriage.

I remember I was about 25 years old and my mother and I had a conversation, she said to me: I apologize to you because I see the same cycle of love you are going through, and I feel it's my fault that you are dealing with this relationship. If I had left your dad a long time ago, you wouldn't think it was normal to stay.

Man, that conversation almost had me in tears because you never know until it's presented to you. I give my mom credit for the apology; sometimes, you will not get that.

You will just get an oh well mentality, but I understand my mother's struggle because she loved my dad and wanted and desired to have a healthy marriage. She fought for her marriage for a very long time.

THROUGH IT ALL

Despite being broken by love countless times, I realized that the people I needed to love me properly didn't know how to. I still have faith that God is going to give me a healthy marriage, and that my husband will value me, appreciate me, and adore me. I didn't trust anyone after the hardship that I had endured because I looked and said How can other people be happy, Why am I'm not married yet? Why can't I get what I deserve, because I know I'm valuable, have a lot to offer, but I had to learn that His will for my life was better than what I desired. I had to let God take complete control over my life and let His will be done because I was and still am completely tired of doing it my way. I have to learn how to trust God in every area of my life.

Matthew 6:33 says Seek ye first the kingdom of God and righteousness, and all these things shall be added unto you.

Can I tell you this is not the easiest thing because our flesh wants what it wants. But God knows what is best. The only thing I would rewind is how I played a part in my level of pain, probably wouldn't have stayed around as long. I would love myself even better. I didn't know my worth at an early age, I learned late, but I know now I'm not settling for anything less than what I deserve. I'm also setting the pavement for my daughters and other women who might have a similar story or pain of rejection from love.

THE PAIN

The level of pain I was enduring from 18 years of the wrong love was so deep, and it cut me to the point I just didn't have faith or wanted to die because I just couldn't understand why. I eventually started doing therapy to figure out if I was the problem or it was my choice of men. I was picking, you know that they say opposite attracts or you end up picking the same man as your dad. I would pick the men I know weren't my type, but shoot. I still feel like I lost. But at the end of the day, God's hand was on my life the whole time because it was so real. I was also wondering who would take care of my daughters. It will be selfish of me to want to take my life because two men I loved so deeply hurt me so deeply. I know now God is a restorer, a deliverer, He will turn this pain into purpose, even when I didn't feel that way. To be honest, I still feel lost because I'm still waiting on God's promise for my life, and that is to have a great, successful, and healthy marriage. His words say in,

Isaiah 61:3 I will turn beauty for ashes in time of sorrow, pain.

I'm a living testimony of that because I'm sitting here writing a book of my pain. Can I be honest? I was embarrassed because I didn't want to look like I couldn't keep a man or that there was something wrong with me.

FAITH

Hebrew 11:1 Faith is the substance of things hoped for and evidence of things not seen.

I see myself getting married to who God has ordained to be my husband. But at this moment in my life, to be honest, I'm a bit fearful and nervous because I have been through turmoil in my relationships. With how other situations didn't work out for me, I just have to keep holding on to God's unchanging hand. He is not a man who should lie. I just have to keep going, hold on to the horns of the altar, because let me tell you, this dating scene nowadays is horrible. You don't know what you are dealing with, and what people's intentions are. That's where praying and faith come in, because I want people's true intentions to come out and to have them revealed in the beginning, instead of when my feelings get involved. Yes, I know y'all are probably thinking. How can I keep my faith? Well, for one, I had too many hang ups on relationships along with failed ones. So much that I have to trust that God will give me better because his plan for our life is good, not evil. God loves me and wants me to have better and be great, it's not easy.

THERAPY

Therapy helped a lot in digging into some wounds that needed to be healed from. Sometimes, when we endure so much trauma and pain, we mask it, we cover. It also gets swept under the rug as though everything is ok, and we are all right. Truth be told, we are not all mentally good. In order for us to be healed correctly, we have to dig from the roots of the pain and trauma to help us recognize the problem, so we don't repeat or fall into the same cycle. According to the Scriptures, our portion is for us to have life and have it more abundantly. All the riches in the world can't heal the wound, but therapy, having faith in God, and trusting his plan will help heal. As I mentioned earlier, I refuse to be stuck, bitter, and miserable because of someone else's mistake. Let's take our power back, ladies. I refuse to be miserable, I deserve true love and happiness. I will get it, and you ladies will receive it. I'm not dying unhappy for nobody.

DISPOSABLE

Just writing this book is showing me how people can dispose of you in their life when they never had genuine pure love. When trauma has come into their life, when they never dealt with the issues of hurt, etc in their life, they bleed on you and don't know they do. But it is up to us to recognize the patterns and correct the behavior. I explained a lot of my life, but there was some more stuff I wanted to write, I didn't want this book to be too long. I'm a straight to the point person. Just know we have a cross to bear, it's all about how we go about and carry that cross, trials and tribulations. But it's up to us how we handle and carry ourselves. When you walk with God, you will suffer. But when suffering, He keeps you in His hands because my suffering could have been a lot worse. We have more strength than what we think. He gives us strength like never before. I could've turned to drugs, alcohol, become a man eater or just running from men because I don't trust them.

STRENGTH

Ladies, we carry children for 9 months, we push them out, we raise our children, we wear so many hats. God will help us carry the weight of the world. It's not easy, but it's our duty to carry our family to help our men/husband to become better leaders. So when we endure just know, it's because we have the strength.

Luke 12:48 to whom much is given much is required.

I'm not saying we should endure pain after pain, but we have to endure hardship so we can wear our crowns.

WAR OF LOVE

1 Corinthians 13:4 Love is patient, kind does not envy or boast.

Just now at an early age, I didn't know what love is, all I saw was my mom and dad's love, how they fought, argued, and just got married. Also, as I mentioned before I thought that was love, but it wasn't, it was dysfunctional love and what I experienced for 18 years. I didn't know my value, or worth, or even healthy boundaries. What I saw my mother put up with from my dad, I thought it was love, but I wasn't sure why I started this chapter with God's word. We have to identify real love versus toxic love. I know pain is not in vain. I went through this to be stronger.

GOT MY MOJO BACK

Hello, I had to regroup and realign my spirit and soul with God again. I felt so defeated and uneasy, but I still have to know God gives us victory and peace in the midst of a storm.

I had to dig deep within me to not let the enemy slip me into a deep depression because the very thing we desire can do us in. Say someone else who denied you to marry them marries someone else, and a 11-year toxic relationship with my daughter's dad, that is a gut-wrenching painful experience, but I have to know God has better, and I will walk in the promises of God.

Mark 9:24 The scripture says God I believe, but helps my unbelief because circumstances, battles, and storms can knock you down, but it takes a great deal of faith and courage to get back up.

This ties in to one of my favorite movies, Creed II. The story shows how Adonis recovered from losing a boxing match with his opponent through resilience and support from his wife and Coach. The loss broke him down because he wanted to avenge his father's death. But he triumphed after he resolved his emotional battles and fought back with strategy. I see myself in this light, triumphing and having my final victory. The question is, how do I collect myself, and who will be in my corner?

MEETING THE LOVE OF MY LIFE

The love of my life was different. Jason and I met when I was with my ex-fiance Randall, we spoke to each other a few times, but it was nothing major. When I left my ex-fiance about 6 months later we rekindled our friendship, he wasn't ready yet to be in a relationship so we remained friends, but we will see each other from time to time. Feelings started to grow and so by August of 2021, we took our relationship to another level. He moved in. We were good, but I started noticing a change in his behavior. He would stay gone for days, make excuses, and just wanted to distance himself from me.

I started questioning his behavior and we would just argue. So a month before everything hit the fan, God woke me up and told me to take my hands off of him. I said how does that look, he told me to stop reaching out. I did, a week before everything got exposed, I had a dream that I had gotten bitten by a black and yellow spider. The same week of the dream, all of his secrets got exposed. He was living a double life and he was still with his ex and she was pregnant the whole time we were together. Man, I was so devastated and torn again and broken to the point I really didn't want to live. Why do they go on with life and we sit in their trash of betrayal, hurt, pain, lies and deceit?

I was lost, I lost weight, my hair came out, I was not myself at all. My pillars

(my daughters and God) were the only reason I fought because I said What is the point of living if people don't respect you or appreciate or love you the way you desire to be loved, why am I living? Have you ever loved someone so much that you knew this person could have been your soulmate, the most bizarre thing is that he has the same birthday as my daughter's dad. We connected on so many levels, were compatible on so many levels, and the chemistry was unspeakable.

I didn't speak to him for 14 months, in the meanwhile he had another woman who he was with message me on Facebook asking for bail money. I asked her Who are you? And she responded with saying she was his cousin. (She is not!) I didn't send her any money, though he was actually in some trouble.

Around 5 months later, I got a phone call. He had gotten shot 5 times. I was hurt, I wanted to visit him in the hospital to make sure he was ok. I didn't go down there because I was unsure if he was with another woman.

Instead I called the hospital. He was a gunshot victim so I was unable to get any information that way.

5 months after, he hit me up on my messenger on FaceBook, he gave me his number, so I reached out to him, because after everything got exposed, he came and got his clothes, and that was the end of everything. Well, we talked. I explained to him my feelings and how I felt, and everything he apologized about but I felt it wasn't a sincere apology because he felt that the way his life was being lead, with the double life and baby was ok.

He was living with another female at the time we started back talking again. He texted me and said Hey can I stay with you for a few days, my emotions and my heart instantly said yes, but after I responded, I started thinking is this the right move. He ended up staying with me for a whole month. One night he just got irritated out of nowhere, and he left. He was gone for the whole night, we spoke the next day, he started an argument for nothing and said I'm coming to get my stuff. I was hurt. His mother came and picked up his belongings. She apologized, and that was that. I mourned it for a whole month. I healed and started feeling amazing again. Going out, loving myself.

In the midst of all of that, my daughter's dad had gotten into some trouble with the law. In January 2024, my daughter's dad was sentenced to 20 years in prison in Virginia. Man, because the heart I have I was hurt. I said Abba how much more can I take this is way too much. I give up. But I still had to be a mother to my daughters and try to be the best because now, they only have one parent.

AFFLICTION!

Fast forward around 4 months later, I was with my daughters, and out of nowhere, I got sick. I just felt so weak, I vomited and just ate a lot, so I could feel better. A few weeks after that I was sleeping and I woke up out of my sleep with some excruciating pain, and my first thought was Abba, I know I don't have cancer. I remember having a mammogram a few years back, and the doctors would say the first sign of breast cancer is not pain. I went for an OB check-up, and my doctor said it's time for you to get a mammogram. Well, you will guess my age, lol. I had some issues with my breast and my underarm. I felt a lump under my armpit, but thought it was a sweat gland bump.

I proceeded to get a mammogram, and they found two lumps, one in my breast and one under my armpit. They said we need you to come back and get a biopsy. I was scared. I called my Apostle. I said Please pray for me, they found two lumps, and we prayed. The next week I was scheduled for the biopsy, they proceeded with the biopsy, they numb you in the areas where they see the tumor, when the radiologist was doing my biopsy she asked me did they set you up with an oncologist. I said no, was I supposed to? She said we will wait for the results to come back.

April 22, 2024

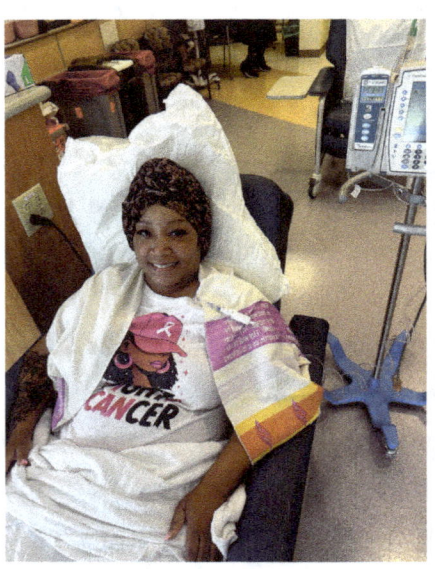

I was diagnosed with the most aggressive breast cancer triple negative, it's the hardest to treat, and treatment is powerful. I started chemotherapy at the end of May, I started getting sick, and my hair fell out in August, right before my birthday. I was devastated. I honestly didn't know how to trust Abba in this process. I never was sick, I worked out and ate healthy for the most part. As I'm writing this I am in tears and anger because I don't know why I was picked for all these battles and war. To see me be transformed from my regular self to someone I didn't even recognize, but I kept fighting and believing when I didn't know how to believe Abba on this level of sickness and despair, I trusted him on healing me from heartbreak, but not on healing me from cancer. Abba healed me from cancer in a few months, I will be a one year survivor. Hallelujah, he will do it because it could have gone another way. I'm here still writing and telling my story of when a woman is broken.

THINKING

I continue to write and encourage women to be strong. This is a challenging task for me because I felt defeated holding on to God's promise and having faith while nothing is adding up. It will knock you off your feet and cause you to give up, and not want you to do anything but just exist. One thing about me: I'm very honest with my feelings and how I feel about my walk with God and the measure of my faith. But my readers are going through this journey with me. I appreciate that right now, my faith is shaky, and the unknown of my next chapter is scary. I'm hurting as I write this book. I was encouraged. I relived some past painful experiences while writing. Now I'm hurt, partially broken, but we will get through this.

I REFUSE TO BE BROKEN

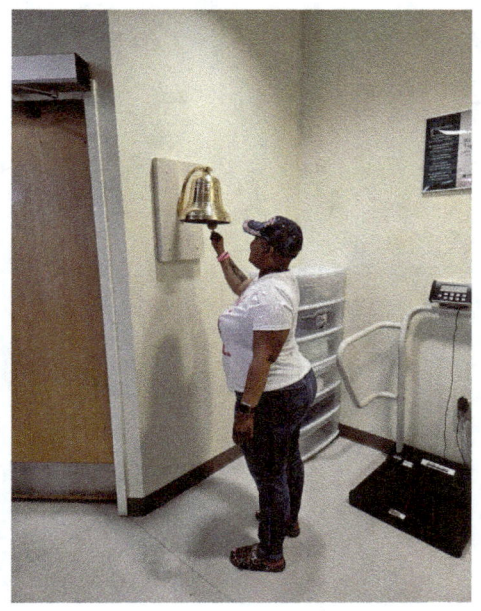

I love that new song by Beyoncé. The title alone speaks volumes: "Break my soul." I'm not allowing other people's actions, motives, and agendas to break my soul. I see myself as victorious and an overcomer. God has so much in store for me to get done while I'm here on this earth. That's going to be my main focus while arriving at a few of my destinations. I know this is a short chapter, but it's real, and God gives us dominion over the earth, so I'm ready. I want my woman to be ready with me.

GUESS WHO'S BACK?

I took three months off to regroup, enjoy the summer, and figure my life out and laugh out loud. I had a lot going on, but I'm much better. I was trying to figure out how I should finish the book, maybe with a bang, and just to be in good spirits no matter what life may bring. I know one thing, the hardest thing to do is to remain pure at heart and genuine when people you love break and destroy your soul to the core. How can you receive love after so many disappointments from past relationships? I wanted to hate them, but God wouldn't allow that, and I didn't want to remain stuck. I just knew what God has for me is bigger and better than I could imagine.

I'M GLAD I'M STILL STANDING

I love Marvin Sapp's song " My testimony." He speaks to my spirit and my soul because we live in a broken world. We are going to endure pain just to hold on to the horns of the altar. As my former Bishop says all the time, life can get real in the blink of an eye. I just want to tell my women to stay encouraged, keep your faith, and know God loves you. We are the apple of his eye, my passion and my purpose is to help and encourage my other women.

This book is for everyone, because you came in contact with it, man or woman. But this book is written for my ladies in mind. No disrespect to the men, but God gave me this book to encourage and inspire women. I just pray it helps to heal and deliver someone, because if I can change one life or encourage them to believe in God and his son, then I have done my job.

I'm humbled that God gave me the vision to write this book and pour into his precious women.

www.ingramcontent.com/pod-product-compliance
Lightning Source LLC
Chambersburg PA
CBHW052123070526
44586CB00016B/2053